Letters from My Wife

Datron Gillon

ISBN-978-1-960853-58-5

Liberation's Publishing LLC
Columbus - Mississippi

Letters from My Wife

Dear Reader,

First, of all I want to say, "Thank You." Thank you for allowing me to live out my dream. I truly can't explain how appreciative I am for your love, support, and encouragement. You are a big part of why we're here and why this book is in your hand. You're a big part of why I finally broke out of my shell. You made this possible and that is why I say thank you.

What you have in your hand are letters that tell the story of a woman who had to live life without her future husband, the father of her then one year old son. These letters tell the ups and downs, victories and defeats that they shared. What you're going to read will read like something you've heard before, simply because it's nothing out of the ordinary. It may sound like so many other's stories, but there is one major difference. It's HER story. Who is the her I'm writing of? It is none other than my wife. Jamara Gillon.

Welcome to "Letters from My Wife" I pray you enjoy every word and feel every emotion. And, see the Faith that took us both through one of the most trying times of our lives!

Letters from My Wife

King!

Hey Babe! Miss you and LOVE you so much! I have been thinking about you like crazy since I last saw you. HAPPY BIRTHDAY!!! Babe I can't believe you're 25. Another year with you is the best thing ever! This is a step to seeing your fantasy of us getting old together! I can't wait either! As long as I'm with you, there is nothing better!

The deal with the phone— I see you called Saturday, and I'm not sure what happened! I called and talked to Mrs. Martin on Friday. She added me onto the list, and I told her that my phone didn't accept collect charges. So, she said I had to call for the prepaid thing. She gave me the number. I called, gave the woman my debit card information, and they charged $25 and said that was about 4 or 5 calls. I'm calling back ASAP to see what's up. Just keep trying all this week! Call me anytime before 4pm. I don't have to be at work until 5pm. They cut my hours all the way down! That's another story I'll tell you all about when I come see you!

The girls haven't really said anything to me about coming to see you! Nickie said Vamp trying to get his stuff together to come with me! So, we'll see! Anyway HAPPY 25TH BIRTHDAY!!!! I love you more than you'll ever know!

Letters from My Wife

My Love,

Philippians 1:6 says, Being confident of this very thing. That he which hasth begun the good work in you will perform it until the day of Jesus Christ.

My goal up until you come home (but really for the rest of our life) is to keep you encouraged every day! This scripture is written by Paul (some say along with Timothy or Timothy acted as a secretary alongside Paul) to the church at Philippi. In the beginning of this chapter, Paul is encouraging the church (even though they were a church out of order). He goes on to thank them and to let them know that they are always in his prayers. When it gets to verse 6 Paul was led to encourage. What I take from the scripture is that Paul was assured that when God blesses you with a good work that He will continue that good work in you until His return, developing that good work, perfecting that good work, and bringing it to full completion for you. So whatever idea that God gives you, never ever allow anyone, not even me to get in the way of Him giving you all the means to fulfill it. He will give you all the necessary tools.

So, I want to encourage you to continue writing about opening a lawn care service. We write music, car raffle, and most importantly preaching the Gospel. I may not say all the necessary words when you need it. I am your biggest cheerleader. I love you, be encouraged to continue to pray.

XOXO
Love You
Mrs. Gillon

Letters from My Wife

3

King

Hey Sweetheart, Just want to start off by saying that. I hope and pray that this letter finds you in the best health and spirit, and of course I hope that I bring a smile to your face. 7-14-85 was the day a King was born. You would be with me forever. Even in the circumstances we are in being separated. It feels like we are closer than every ------->

Hey Datron I told your wife to quit writing so I could sing. well write. HAPPY BIRTHDAY 2 U. HAPPY BIRTHDAY 2 U! HAPPY BIRTHDAY 2 U BRO LAW. HAPPY BIRTHDAY 2 UUUUUU.

O yea! this is Mica Hope all is well with you. Luv u bunches!

Well this is me again. I pray this gets to you in time for your birthday. Your birthday is supposed to be filled with joy, and you are supposed to feel special. I hope I did that. Not only on your birthday, but everyday. I miss you so much and you will get THE REAL GIFT, Saturday. I love you and can't wait to see you!

Your Wife
Jamara Gillon

PS. 1+1=2 I love you!

Letters from My Wife

To My King: Datron Devaughn Gillon

Hey Sweetheart! How are you doing? Well first, I've been waiting on those 4 words for 7 years! (Will you marry me?) YES YES YES YES! of Course I'll marry you. I hope I filled all the information out correctly on the application. What do we do about rings? Do I need to get those or will they be provided? What do I do about getting our blood work done? Nickie said they are supposed to send me some form for getting blood taken!? then I am supposed to get fax it to Green County. I don't know, but I'm so excited! When I got the application in the mail I just started jumping for joy! I am so ready for this! I told the family. They said what they had to say, but it's all about me and you not about what everyone else thinks. If I have anything else I need to do or fill out go ahead and sent it back ASAP! (Got that from you)!

Love you!
Write back soon!
I'm excited!
Your Wife Jamara Gillon!

Letters from My Wife

5

Datron Devaughn Gillon

What's going on guy! I got your letter after I had already sent my letter off. I was so happy to hear from you. I know that the letter I sent you before was a little sad, but at the time I wrote the letter, I was really down and out. I thought for days to not even send that letter. I knew it would make you sad! But, you're the only one that I can talk to. I miss you so much. I still feel guilty, because I feel like I need to get you here. I know there is nothing I can do about it. It hurts.! Your letter that I got about us being together for 7yrs was so sweet! It made me cry. After seven years of being together you still know how to make me feel good when I'm feeling bad. I'm so lucky to have you. You've grown so much! I'm coming to see you as soon as I can. More than likely it will be towards the end of January or beginning of February.

Seeing you will help my sick soul also! That's all I need is to see you! I miss you so much. Dook is doing good. He's getting bigger and badder every day! He is what's keeping me going most days. I'll be moving soon. I thought about moving down that way, but it will be my luck that you get moved if I do come. When this year comes in I'm going to try my best to come see you once a month. Hope to see you soon!

Your Queen
~Jamara Gillon~
Happy 7th to you too!

Letters from My Wife

Datron Devaughn Gillon (MY KING)

Hey Sweetheart! How are you? Better, I hope! First & foremost, I want you to know that I love and miss you more than words can describe. But I know it ain't nothing but the Good Lord that's keeping me going. Sometimes I let the Devil get the best of me. But the Lord always over powers him and lifts me up! Once again, I'm only human and we tend to get like that.

Once again we tried to come see you. I started to strike out by myself, but me and Dook on the highway for 4 1/2 hours is not a good look! Try to get moved closer to home whenever you can, because Leakesville is a long way from here. I know you worry about me, but don't (Which I know you can't help it!) Everything is going to be better for me (us) real soon. I believe that in my heart! What I want you to do is keep your head up! Keep praying for us. This is just a test!

The Lord has revealed so much to me, especially in these last past few days. Do you remember that letter you wrote me saying everything is going to get better? Sometimes it seems like you're living right and praying and nothing seems to go your way. The sinner next to me seems to have everything he wants. That's how I was feeling, but the Lord revealed to me that there is a time and a season for everything. Even though I already know that, it's a difference. I want you to hold on and believe. I know times get hard, and it seems like you want to give up, but hold on. Don't fall into the devil's trap. Stay strong, because that's what keeps me going everyday. It's a daily process. That's how I live day by day. Think on the good things! I love you!

Your First Lady!
Jamara Asha Gillon

Letters from My Wife

To My Baby:

Hey! How are you doing? Fine I hope! If you're mad at me for my phone being off and not writing all this time, I can understand. I have been going through a lot lately, but everything is much better now. I really don't want to get into too much, but I've been really down, emotionally, financially, spiritually and physically. God has picked me back up as He always does. I'm much better now. I got a new number, but it want be on until or between the 26th and 30th of next week. So try my number all this upcoming week!

It's a cheaper phone company. Don't feel like the phone being off was all your fault. It was partially mine too. Call as soon as you think the phone is on. I have a lot to tell you that I would rather tell you over the phone than on paper! I have something to ask you. I love you with all my mind, body, & spirit,

Love Your Wife
Jamara

Letters from My Wife

To the Love of my Life, Datron Devaughn Gillon

Hey Sweetheart! How's things going with you? Fine I hope. First & foremost I gotta tell you how much I love you and miss you. I've been a little down lately, but when I finally heard your voice it cheered me up a whole lot. Every time I hear from you it excites my soul, and you always be on time and always know what to say when I feel like I know it all. You encourage me to be a better person. You inspire me to keep on going even when I feel like I can't. I don't know why I let the devil get to me sometimes. It's like he knows my weak spots, and he always tries to get to them. I know He is only trying to tempt me and test me to see if I'm gone fall into his trap. But, I'm stronger than that. I'm stronger than what I thought I was. It surprises me sometimes. When you first left I thought everything was over for me, but I had to step up and I still got to step up. It's so much that I have to learn. Sometimes I feel like I got a big heavy load on my back. I know my God wouldn't put more on me than I can bare! I know God is trying to show how to move from a young lady to a woman. I got to hold on while it's my time to shine. I heard a preacher say, "Hold on for your blessing. Sometimes it could take 3 years for your blessing!" I know my blessing is on its way. I honestly believe that. I just got to build some strength up for the hard times.

Like Joseph prepared all the food for the scarce times that were coming. I got to put my game face on and come to the realization that in reality I got to take care of me and Dook and get over the fact that I got to do it by myself for now. If I don't, I could easily fall back into that same state of mind that I have been in. Every since I talked to you last week I finally put my foot down. I got faith from here on out. Everything is going to get better for every body. Everyone has their time to shine and ours is coming soon! From here until you get home I'm going to have to make decisions as a woman of God and realize what's most important to me! If I can't take care of me first then how am I going to take car of my babies. (You and Dook) Ya'll are the most important people in my life, besides God of Course.

9

Thank you Baby for your words of encouragement! I couldn't make it without you! Even with you physically away from me I can't live without you! Every since I talked to you. I put my business suit on Baby! I'm on my grown woman! Come on home to me Daddy! Don't have me waiting too long! Call me soon!

Love You Always
Your Wife
Jamara Asha Gillon

Letters from My Wife

Datron Devaughn Gillon

Hey Sweetheart! How are you doing? Good I hope! Me? I'm blessed as I can be! If you didn't already know, I'm gone; not for good because I still got some business to handle. This is more of a vacation right now. Nickie called me and told me the scoop! I've been waiting on that phone call so I can send you that issue. It's okay here where I'm at. It reminds me too much of Amory. Not that I hate Amory, it's just that I moved to better myself and jobs are scarce just like they are in Amory. I'm thinking about moving to Memphis with Nette! It's just 45 minutes away! Everything is good though! No more stressing this year! So if you already done wrote me, I'm going to Amory sometimes this week to get my mail transferred.

Whatever address I use when I write, use that one because they talking about moving! Baby I miss you so much. I can't wait to see you again especially when we were able to get conjugal visits. I love you so much! I can't wait to marry you. I'm so anxious. I just thought I'd write you to give you an update on me and Dook! Write me back soon!

Jamara Stallings Gillon

Letters from My Wife

To My Love

Hey Sweetheart, how are you doing today? Good I hope. I'm blessed as I can be with this marriage license paper. I was not sure on the part that I filled out. I went to the courthouse, but they told me that I would have to go to Greene County. I've been trying to get in contact with your case manager, but it's been like pulling teeth to get in touch with her and I still haven't. So I filled out the paper anyway, because I didn't want to be too late on getting it sent back in. So, talk to her and see what I have to do. I'm so excited. I'm nervous that I might mess something up with the papers. I can't wait til I say "I do!"

You know that phone call I had been waiting on about that, "thang thang" I did get it, but she was beating around the bush and said she was gone call me back, but she never did. So you need to come up with a plan B. Until then, I want you to call my cell phone. I'm going to set up a prepay account so I can talk to you at least once a week. This is killing me that I can't talk to you. I love you. I miss you!

Your wife
Jamara Asha Gillon

Letters from My Wife

My Love

Hope you had an awesome birthday! I still want to say I'm sorry for not mailing them off on time for your birthday. I love you so much, and I really hope and pray this is your last birthday behind bars. I have been feeling some type of way without you being here on your birthday. I get like that on every birthday and holiday. It made me miss you even more. I love you so much and can't wait to see you. There will not be any money on the phone Friday, (I'm so sorry) But, funds are low and school is right around the corner. See you Saturday. Call me Friday (Phone tap me) just to say I love you. I need to hear your voice. You can do it a few times.

Wifey
Mrs. Gillon

Letters from My Wife

To My King Datron Devaughn Gillon

Hey Sweetheart! How's it going? Hopefully good! Baby I miss and love you more than you'll every know! I hope everything goes through with the marriage because, I'm so ready to officially be Jamara Asha Gillon! Just writing that makes me excited inside. After talking to you it reassures me why I love you so much! I'm gone keep it a secret, because I don't want it to go to your head! LOL! Today is Sunday August 23. I just felt like today was gone be a great day, but it's just ok. I'm thankful that I woke up this morning and for all HIS many blessings.

Once you have that experience of having your own you don't ever want to have to fall back and depend on nobody else. It's tough sometimes, but when you make a move like I did, you have to deal with the consequences! On another note: I'm so happy that you are so close to me. You know Bo is coming to all of your visitations. You know ain't no getting around her! LOL! Now when we get married I'm gone have to tell her. LOL. Baby you are my best friend. It was a lot on my mind today and I just got to writing! I know I can always come to you for anything. I thank you for always being there for me when I have needed you the most and always being an ear, even when we used to be mad at each other. That lets me know that you really care! (That's one reason I love you so much) It's this song by Beyoncé that's called "I'd rather go blind." I listened to it all last night and today! The song is saying that she would rather be BLIND than to SEE her man leave her. It's a beautiful song. That's exactly how I feel when I come see you, and then turn around and have to leave you!

That's the worst part of visitation to me. Man you got my head gone! What did you do to me? Hypnotize me? LOL Do you got me under a spell? If you do just let me know! LOL. Real talk though! I love you with all my heart!
XOXO Hugs & Kisses
See you soon!

Letters from My Wife

14

Hey Sweetheart!

How are you doing? Good I hope! Me? I'm ok. I could be doing a whole lot better. As you can see this letter has my sister Nette address on it. That means I live here now! I'm okay so don't worry, Jasmine did send me your letter, but I got it too late to do that summer package. So I'll just send you the money instead, other than that, everything is good. We still coming to see you on the 11th. Its supposed to be me, Tip, Bo, and Jeremiah. So if you haven't turned Tip's visitation form in, please do so. HAPPY FATHER'S DAY. I know I'm late, but it's all good! I know you would be the best if you were here. I miss you & I love you!

Jamara Asha Gillon

Letters from My Wife

To my love,

Hey sweetheart! How are things going with you. Hopefully this letter finds you in good spirits. Sorry it took so long to write you! I miss you so much! Me and Bo are making plans to come see you in July around your B'day! Everybody is doing good around my way. Jerry is getting bigger and badder everyday. He misses his daddy though. Every time he see your picture he still knows who you are, but he'll say he want to come over your house! He so grown now. He's in Amory right now and been down there for two weeks and I miss him like crazy too. I'm going to get him on my next off day. He'll be starting school in August and I'm gone be happy and sad at the same time. I can't believe he's about to be 4! Time has really been flying. I miss you so much! There's not a day that goes by that I don't think about you! I've been having dreams that you are here. Dreams really do mean things! So maybe your time will be coming to an end soon. I can't wait for that day! I miss you so much. I can't wait to come see you.

You can send me that summer package. I'll pay for it since I haven't sent you any money in a while. I apologize. I'm just now getting on my feet a little. I can't wait to see you. I miss you so much and Love you!
Keep your head up!
Your Wife Jamara Gillon

PS> What's up with you getting transferred closer to home? Write back ASAP!

Letters from My Wife

Datron Devaughn Gillon

Hey Sweetheart! How are things going with you? Good I hope. I'm missing you like crazy right now. I've got a good feeling about you coming home soon! I done prayed and prayed on it. I'm feeling really confident that everything gone work out in our advantage. I'm gone try my best to get a phone so you can call home. It's killing me that I can't talk to you! Everything is good my way, I can't complain about nothing; I'm blessed as I can be. Even with me complaining all the time about the thing I say I need. I know the Lord gone bless me when He thinks it's best for me to have those things. I can't complain. My life is good right now. It would just be better if you were here! Man I really do miss you and Love you dearly. Hurry up and get back to me! I need you bad! I hope my letter finds you in good spirits. Stay up! & be blessed! We love you! Me and Dook!

Yours Truly,
Jamara Stallings Gillon

Letters from My Wife

Datron Devaughn Gillon

Hey Sweetheart! How are you doing? Better I hope. Me? I'm better! I apologize for taking forever to write you back! Your cards were so beautiful that you sent me. Thank you. Where do I start with everything? There is so much to catch you up on. First of all, I got a job at a Dollar General Store. I've been there for about two weeks. It's an ok job. It's nothing I want to be doing, but it is a job. Another thing is Nette won me and her third row tickets to a Lil' Wayne, T-pain and Keri Hilson concert. It was so fun! I got pictures and I'll be sure to send you some. On to you. I will send you fifty dollars for your fan. I might have to send twenty-five dollars twice, if that's ok. I know you want to see me & I want to see you just as bad. Right now It's hard for me to see you. The money is not an issue. It's the fact that I don't have a car. The Cadillac is over. I left the "Lac" back in Amory broke down! Even though I have my driver's license, nobody is willing to let me drive their car that far.

I've been trying to get down there since I've been here. The first chance I get though baby, I promise I'll be to see you. I know you don't want to be transferred anywhere, but if that means that you'll be closer to home, then that's a better chance you'll get more visits. But like you said, it's all in God's hands! That's where I try to keep everything. Even though it gets hard sometimes, I'm missing you like crazy right now! Sometimes I'll slide into a depressed state of mind. I still can't believe that you've been gone this long. I'm still here. Alive. I never thought that I would make it this long without you right here with me. I thought by now I would have lost my mind, but it had to have been God in Control. I'm still kind of sad that we want be getting married this May. I'm so sad right now too baby. Seeing you is all my sad soul needs. I'm go try my best to come see you at the end of this month or the 1st of May. Just hang tight baby, I'm gone pull some strings for you! Hold on!
I love you. I miss you!
your Wife
Jamara Asha Gillon

Letters from My Wife

18

To My King!

Hey Sweetheart! Glad to hear the good news about you being transferred. That's going to be so much better for the both of us. Now with the marriage, you know me, the sooner the better! Right now I don't know if I can make that trip to Leakesville, because 1st I don't have a ride, and second I don't have a dime unless Bo would be willing to bring me. If I'm not able to come before you get moved, we'll just have to wait until you get moved to Marshall County. From here to Holly Springs ain't nothing but about 30 minutes. So it shouldn't be a problem! Everything's gone work, out because I done gave it all up to the man upstairs! I got some good news! I had an interview for a job on last Thursday. They called me back and asked would I be interested in the job. The job is being an insurance agent through Liberty National Insurance. It's really good money (Great Money!) I have to take a seven day class and pass the test in order to be licensed. You have to be licensed to sale insurance. It's a really good work environment.

The class is gone cost me $69 to sign up and take the test for my certification. I see my future with good things in it. I think we gone be alright! Pray for me that everything goes ok. Which I know it will! Just hold on and be patient. When I get on my feet, I'm really gone be on my feet. Soon as I start working. I'm already gone have my apartment because Nette know a friend that is the manager over some apartments, and the job is not far from where I'm going be staying (and Wal-Mart is right around the corner) (My favorite store) LOL!

Undra said for me not to worry about a ride! He gone let me use one of the vehicles they don't drive until I'm able to get what I want. Don't worry Baby I'm gone get something nice (I deserve it) I think everything gone be alright for Jamara Asha Stalllings Gillon! (I will take the Stallings off when it's official) Pray for me!

I called down there, and I couldn't get in touch with that lady. It is so hard to try to talk to somebody, because a machine answers the phone. Then, somebody will transfer, if nobody answers, it will go back to the machine. It's complicated! But it will work out soon.

19

I love you! I miss you! I can't wait to see you. Thank you for being who you are. Always giving me the strength when usually it's the other way around! Stay Strong and stay encouraged! I love you!
Your First Lady
Jamar Asha Gillon

PS. Write back ASAP & let me know when you get moved, so I can come see you. I got a lot of pictures. I'm gone send them but I just ain't got the funds to send them right now. They'll be coming soon though.

Letters from My Wife

My Love,

I just want to start off by saying I love you, and I miss you terribly! This has been a tough week for me. The fact that my visit was cut short only being allowed two hours of visitation. I cannot wait until this journey is over! Some of these people at the prison thrive off of making other people's lives miserable. I understand that they have rules to follow, but they make up rules as they go. Every week it's something different. They only allow us two hours of visitation because of over crowdedness, but allow people coming in at 12 o'clock three hours. They are never fair! Then said I saw you the day before, and that was a privileges'! Ridiculous! They make up their own rules! I called the warden and it was like talking to one of my kindergartners! I'm giving this to God, because I was filled with so much anger and frustration

Love your wife!
Jamara Asha Gillon!

Letters from My Wife

King!

Hey King! Sitting here at work kind of bored. Still HIGH and on cloud 9 from our visit this past Sunday! Baby you are the truth, and that's all I'm gone say!!! I love you more than you'll every know. I love being in your presence! I can honestly say that you are my best friend! I fall in love with you more and more every time we're together! Baby words can't express the feelings I have for you! YOU ARE THE MAN!!! I'm so proud of you and all of your endeavors. I can't wait until you get home and start leading people to salvation. I'm gone be right there beside you every step of the way. Baby I applied for school, and I did my financial aid which gone pay for school. I have to go to ICC next week to get my classes for the fall semester! Baby just filling out the ICC application and financial aid application made me so excited! It feels so right this time. I can't wait! I have so much motivation! Baby the future is looking great! When I get them nursing license, I'm gone start looking for jobs and schools for Dook! I can't wait! For once in my life it really seems like everything is going to be aright.

Thank you so much for being who you are in my life! I thank God for you everyday all day! You might not feel like you're working, but you are! You are the MAN! I LOVE YOUR words of encouragement. Just talking to you about everything makes all the pain go away! You're like my personal drug! [I could have had the worst week every] When I come see you, you only have to say one word and that's "Baby it's gone be alright." Just hearing those words from you gives me that confidence! I love you for that! Babe I still really don't know if I'm gone make it third Saturday. My supervisor still ain't said nothing about it! If I do come the triplets are supposed to come! So, if I come and they come with me, what do you want to do? This is the last visit they will have before they go to school. So, I guess I'll let them make it. So if the girls want to see you, I really don't know. I'm gone try my best to come, because it would kill me to not be able to see you! A whole month will have passed. No way!

The way I'm feeling right now, just let the girls come with me and still get a conjugal visit. I mean what's the worst that could happen! Baby you was so right! That time we have in private is very valuable to me! We'll see! I love you.

Love Your Wife
Jamara Gillon

PS. I still haven't talked to your grandma yet! I'm still praying about it trying to figure it out. Pray for me.
My phone has to be set up like pre-paid. I have to call Global Link and Pay them before you call!

Letters from My Wife

King

How are you today? Good I hope! First and most important, I want to say that I love you very much. Being married to you just made me fall more in love with you. It's a feeling that just overwhelms me. I can't even explain it. Being around you is like being around my best friend who I haven't seen in years. I'm so comfortable with you. I feel protected when I'm with you. It feels like we're one soul. It's so overwhelming. It makes me want to scream for joy and cry at the same time! That's how much I love you. I can't explain it. I've been thinking about you like crazy every since our visit. Even though you made me "MAD" for us not getting a conjugal visit! Naw! Just playing. I really want to come every visit, but I might not get a chance to come every 3rd Saturday! I've asked, but they haven't got back with me. I promise I'll let you know ahead of time. I don't want you to get in trouble for turning in a conjugal visit and you don't actually get one. So I Promise I'll let you know if I'm coming, because I really don't know if I'll be able to come.

Question? Is VAMP's visit approved? Let me know AsAP. He said he would start coming with me. So that way I'll have someone to keep Dook! WRITE me back ASAP to let me know if Vamp visit was approved! I got your letter. Every time I get your letters it just makes me super happy. Thanks for all your advice! I'm taking it all in and putting it into action. On my way home from our visit, I was talking to the Lord. I was thanking Him over and over for having you in my life. You are the Truth Datron Devaughn Gillon. I'm so proud of you and all your endeavors. I wished I was there to hear you bring your first WORD. I can't wait until you get home to be there for you, learn from you, and support you in every way. I love you so much! I can't wait until the 1st Sunday. I can hardly wait. It took a whole week for me the first visit we got for me to calm down LOL. Anyway I love you, Miss you & can't wait to see you.

I love you! Your wife,
Jamara Asha Gillon

PS. Write Back ASAP. Let me know if Vamp's visit was approved!!! They say Vanessa was trying to call to see if the girls visit was approved! I told them yeah though they might want to hear it from you!

Letters from My Wife

My Sweetheart,

How are you doing? Good I hope! I love you and miss you so much. All the famous words in the dictionary can't help me explain the way I feel. I think about you 24/7. It's like you're stuck in my brain. I pray so hard for you, sometimes I cry, but I really feel like God really hears my prayer & He's going to make them come true real soon. I belief that! I heard that Ginuwine song the other day "Better Half" Some people don't know the real true meaning of those words. Some people think it just mean their significant other, (boyfriend or girlfriend) or someone that they love. Well better half to me means the other side of your body that makes it complete or whole! When I think of better halves it's like I can feel your heart, your pain, your excitement, your joy. All the things you're feeling. It seems like I can feel it too. Even when we're not together like right now! This separation from each other has taught me a whole lot. It has taught me independency, self control, and #1 how depending on GOD first and foremost. When you were here I relied on you for for just about everything instead of GOD. I spent 99% of the time with you instead of God. Now being mature my eyes have opened & I see that God comes first. Then my family. So it's a lesson learned & it's time for you to come home. I love and miss you. Dook says, "Wassup Mane!" LOL!

Love you Lots'
Your Wife
Jamara Asha Gillon

Letters from My Wife

King

Hey sweetheart first and foremost I hope and pray this letter finds you in the best of health and spirit. I love and miss you. Well as you know April is now one of my favorite months. It is the month God blessed me with the most beautiful soul. A day I will never forget. I am so grateful that God blessed me with a man like you. It is so many women that long for the relationship we have. Our love is so rare. So many people may ask how or why I could love somebody so much when we are in the situation we're in. The answer is simple. It's nothing but the love I have for God. I'm able to give you the love I have for you. 4/19/2010 is a day I will never forget! I love you!

Happy 2nd Anniversary!
Your Wife & First Lady
Jamara Gillon

Letters from My Wife

My love; My king

I pray this letter finds you in the best health and spirit. With a smile on your face. I just want to start off by saying that I love you. The last letters that I wrote I threw them away, because I wanted to spend as much time as possible uplifting, encouraging you, inspiring you and just edifying you in every way possible. Not that those letters were just all negative. It's just they weren't what you needed. I think sometimes we get caught up in a thing like us talking about what we don't like instead of what we like, what we could be better at instead of saying positive and uplifting things. Those are the things that I want to focus on because I know you and I both thrive off of that. Not saying that having those tough conversation aren't necessary at times. I just feel like affirmations bring out the better of both of us. Maybe, just maybe, we won't have to have too many of the tough uncomfortable conversations that leave us feeling like we're not enough or just feeling bad.

Love your wife
Jamara Asha Gillon

Letters from My Wife

MY love,

    I would like to start off by saying Happy Birthday. Twenty-nine, really looks good on you. I am happy to celebrate another year of life with you. I hope and pray that I bring the biggest and brightest smile to your face and much joy in your heart and most importantly LOVE. That is the biggest gift I could ever give you. Nothing materialistic could ever top the love in my heart for you. I truly adore you, when I told you that if you ever step out on what we have that is to say that I don't have faith in you. It is to show you how much faith I have in you now, in us. I hold you to a very high standard in my life. Not to say that you won't make mistakes. So what it all boils down to is that I love you. I adore you. I respect you. I care for you. I miss you. Happy 29th Birthday. Oh how I wish you were with me to celebrate!

Turn UP!!!

Mrs. D Gillon

Letters from My Wife

29

MY love,

I hope and pray that this letter finds you in the best health and spirit. I miss you terribly already. I'm so blessed and thankful for the time that we do get to spend with each other. It's so precious. That is why I slightly understand why you don't want to have certain conversations with me during the time we have with one another. Because of who we are I don't understand. What I can say is that we have come a long way. I love you so much! You are truly my best friend. That is why I feel like I can talk to you about anything. I am going to try my best to write more. I know how much it means to me to get a letter in the mail. So If not more, Here is Dook's schedule.

Saturday January 17 10am (I don't know if he will make this because of his surgery.

Thursday January 22 5:30pm

Saturday January 31 9:00am (We will not have visit 5th weekend

Tuesday February 10 5:30pm

Saturday February 14 9:00am

Saturday February 21 10am

Saturday February 28 9:00am

PS. Let me know what you suggest I do on game days on Saturday.

Letters from My Wife

King,

My love! What a joy it is to be writing you back on this beautiful Thursday morning. I got your letter yesterday and my spirit was just overjoyed after reading it. We have come along way! With God, we can conquer anything. We are a blessed people, and it will stay that way as long as we keep God as the center of our marriage. I know you said I was right about all that I said, but honestly it was the good Lord. He allowed me to say the words and the situation at this particular time for our "Good" He's amazing! We are both growing. Neither one of us have made it. We will continue to grow into grace and the truth and knowledge of the Lord until eternity. I miss you so much. This is going to be a long two weeks. God will see us through. I love you my king. Be blessed and continue to pray for me as I will for you.

The Wife!

J. Gillon

Letters from My Wife

My Love,

What a joy it is to myself to be writing you! I get so much joy and excitement from communicating with you whether it is by letter or phone or in person! I get that feeling with no one else. You are truly my best friend. What an awesome time I had with you this past Saturday. I believe that our love can do so many things for us! I pray that this letter put a smile on your face while reading this as much as I'm smiling writing it. I miss you terribly! I have dreams about you being home, especially lately. I know that is just conformation that you'll be here soon. Boy I can't wait. I know that all the things that's been on me will no longer just be on me! I know because we are children of God. He is going to give us so many blessings, and we are going to be just fine! I pray daily for that day! I got my money. I will put money on the phone and on your books. I will be seeing you soon.

I miss you. I love you. Continue to pray for me, and I will do the same for you.

Your wife
J Gillon

PS. I love you & Dook said he thinks about you everyday when he opens his eyes! (He really said that. LOL! Love you!)

Letters from My Wife

32

King,

Hear ye! Hear ye! My King, my lover, friend, homie. I miss you soooo much already. I have really been thinking about your graduation approaching. I want you to know I'm super proud of you! You have accomplished so much since you've been in prison. I'm at HELL right now. I also want you to forgive me for making things always about me. When you told me about your upcoming graduation, I felt like I didn't know because I never asked you. I am really happy for you. For us! We are both making power moves. I love you and I cannot wait to see you receive that diploma. It's a feeling of over joy right now. God has been so good to us. We are a blessed people. Matthew 6:33 "seek you first the kingdom of God and His righteousness and all these things shall be added unto you." As long as we put God first we can conquer anything. Love you baby. Have a blessed rest of the week! See you soon!

Mrs. Datron Gillon

PS. I love you

Letters from My Wife

King,

    Hey sweetheart! How are you? Good I hope! I pray this letter brings you great joy and put a smile on your face. I miss you dearly. I'm counting down the days to be in your presence one more time this week. It's just you and me!!!

    It seems like we are truly one soul connected together. You are truly my soulmate. When we're together I feel the oneness. It's nobody but God. I love you so much and I apologize for always making you feel that I'm against you. That has been haunting me all week! I promise whatever you tell me from here on out. I will take your word at face value! That is how it is supposed to be and I'm going to change that! I love you. Can't wait to see you.

Love Mrs. Datron Gillon

Letters from My Wife

King,

Hey sweetheart! I hope and pray that this letter finds you in great health and spirit. I'm like you in a way sometimes. I'm at a lost for words when I write you, and I don't know what more to say, but I love and miss you. I really cherish every moment we spend together, and I begin to count down the days as soon as I leave you. I'm in LOVE! You make me feel like I'm 16 again. Just young and in love. I was just laying on the couch on this beautiful Monday morning, and I jumped to write you real quick before the mail ran. I was thinking about you! I will have your pictures later. I Haven't gotten them printed yet. Vamp also told me to tell you that you never did send him another visitation form. The deadline is in a few days. Well, I love you. I miss you.
Love
Mrs. Datron Gillon

PS. I love you x infinity

Letters from My Wife

King,

Hey sweetie! My love, my everything. I just want to thank you. I know you are wondering why I would be thanking you! It's simply because you make this marriage very easy. Most women do not understand why I'm still here with you after so long. Well I've seen women still be mistreated and misused with their husbands, fiancés, and boyfriends behind prison walls. You make it easy for me to be there for you. I just want to say thank you so much for being the man that you have become. It takes a willing heart! I'm honored to be Mrs. Datron Gillon. I feel like a trophy, sometimes. You are such an amazing man. Words just can't express how I truly feel. I can't wait until Saturday to see you, to kiss you and just be in your presence one more time. I love you! Miss you!

Mrs. Datron Gillon

PS. Look on the back,

Letters from My Wife

This is my hand print! Hold my
hand everyday to get by! Love
ya!

King,

Hey sweetheart, I love you. What better way to start this letter. This has been the hardest week not being able to see you. I miss you so much. You are truly my other half. I know that sounds cheesy, but when I'm not with you. I really feel incomplete. I've been just sitting around daydreaming about your smile. How your teeth look when you smile, your soft lips. Your frame when I'm hugging you. Your hands your gentle caress. The way you look when you're turned on, it lets me know that you want me. I'm in love with you, totally. I feel like our love is a bottomless pit. I just keep falling more and more in love with you. I see a Godly man when I see you, and that makes me feel like if I fall you will catch me. My whole heart trusts and believes you and in you. I want to be your every woman because you make being a woman and a wife so easy. I love you! Can't wait to see you.

Mrs. Gillon

King,

Hey sweetheart, I pray this letter finds you in the best spirit. I just want to start off by saying I love you, and I miss you! I'm sorry your letter did not get sent off earlier. The fact that you needed those addresses. It has been a crazy busy week. I can't wait to see you this Saturday. I know you are glad to be getting these pictures. I promise I'm gone do better on sending you letters and pictures. I just bought a book of stamps and envelopes. So, no excuses. Please forgive me for the slack. God bless and I can't wait until Saturday. I love you with all my heart!

Your Wife
1st Lady
Jamara Gillon

Letters from My Wife

Datron, King

How are you? I know you're super blessed right now to be hearing from me and finally getting the pictures. I can just see your big Kool-Aid smile. I love you so much and miss you so much. I know you are not going to get this until after our visit, because today is Thursdays! See you soon!

Love you!
The Wife
Jamara

Letters from My Wife

40

King

Hey Sweetheart! How are you? I hope and pray this letter finds you in the best health and spirit. Sorry it took a minute to write you back. I was definitely the hold up, because Dook wrote you back the minute he got your last letter. Sorry there are still no pictures. My next class don't start until next Tuesday, so I will print them off later this week. I turned in my final paper, Monday. Pray I did well. I go to the doctor's Wednesday to get a check up to make sure everything is ok.

They will take skin to test for any abnormalities so be in prayer. If you get this letter in time, don't worry about me coming Sunday. I can come Saturday. I want to sneak in town Sunday to see my grandma (Pastor Corine). She called me Monday updating me on the church. She said she's ok. But you know she ain't! I want to surprise her at church Sunday. I now that will bring a smile to her face. If it's too late. I'll wait until next week. Love you! See you soon!

First Lady
J Gillon

Letters from My Wife

King

    Hey Sweety! How are you? Great I hope. I hope and pray that this letter finds you in great health and spirit. I just want to tell you after spending time with you last Saturday. I fell deeper in love with you. I don't know what was the difference, but it has had me on cloud nine all week. When we made love it was a closeness that I felt and I can't explain it. It was amazing. I'm so in love with you. Our love just keep amazing me. I really would rather see you by myself this upcoming week, but Tip and Danielle already sliced up and told me so that wouldn't be fair or nice to tell them. they can't go at the last minute. Tip told me that they supposed to ride with Bo. So look out for a crew! LOL. We'll get alone time soon! Love you!
                      Jamara

Letters from My Wife

King

Hey Sweetheart! How are you? Great I hope I pray this letter find you in great health and Spirit or somehow bring a smile to your face and brighten your day. My King, my king, Where do I begin? Well first I love you and miss you terribly. I have truly been enjoying our past conversations about life and just being able to talk to you about anything is truly a blessing! I want to thank you for your WORD from GOD. You don't know how you have blessed my spirit when you explained to me that when you are in the presence of God there is no sin. Though we may not be perfect it does not excuse us to sin. Imperfections and sin are two totally different words/meanings. This has really been in my spirit every since you asked me. Is it possible to go day by day without singing? Yes it is!!! I think people use "Nobody's Perfect" as a crutch to sin! I think I done asked a 100 people this question. Some say it's up to the individual some say "nobody's" perfect, but thank you for bringing me to realize the truth.

I have a question for you when you call on Friday. (If I ain't asked you already) God Bless. Talk to you later. I LOVE YOU.

Wife & First Lady

XOXOXO

Jamara Asha Gillon

Letters from My Wife

King

Hey Sweetheart! I pray this letter finds you in wonderful health and spirit. I love you and miss you dearly. I am counting down the days that I will be able to hold you, kiss you, and just to be in your total presence. I cherish every moment with you down to the very second. Nothing in this world is better than being your wife. Holding down WIFE, is a marvelous title. It is my absolute pleasure. I think GOD has revealed my calling... mentoring young women and teenaged girls. Pray for me and give me advice on it, and we will talk about it at visit. I also want you to be encouraged. Everything is in God's hands. Don't worry about anything at all! Love You!

First Lady
Jamara Gillon

Letters from My Wife

My Love King

Hello my love! How are you? Great I hope. I pray that this letter finds you in the best of health and spirits. I just want to start off by saying that I love you and miss you dearly. You have really been on my mind heavy since our last visit. I'm sorry it took so long to write you back. This has been a crazy week. Both Monday and Tuesday. We had a youth revival in which I was the MC both nights. We had to help out getting the program together. I typed up the programs and the invitations and passed them out to church.

I have rescheduled my appointment to see the doctor. So be praying for that. Oh yeah, I apologized for not having money on the phone last Friday. It really hurt me that I wasn't able to talk to you. And I know it was very hurting to you as well. I miss you so very much, and I can't wait to see you Saturday. God bless you. Love you & see you soon.

First Lady
Mrs. Gillon

PS. I love you. Please respond to my last set of questions. Thanks!

Letters from My Wife

King

Hey Sweetheart how are you? Great hopefully praying that this letter find you in great health and spirits. Well it is the day after visitation, and I am still high from you. You are THE MAN! I just absolutely love being around you. Being in your presence just makes my heart constantly skip beats. You are the Love of my life and the man of my dreams. I love how we talked all visit and chopped it up like we were best friends. I love your authority. Your intelligence and your opinion as THE MAN. Thank you for all your words of encouragement. Sometimes I need that push I honestly don't know what I would do without you. Sometimes it may seem that I reject you or what you tell me, but when I think about it, you give me nothing but the truth. Thank you for calling and talking to Jasmine. Whatever decision you make, I'm with you. I love you! I miss you already.

First Lady
Jamara Gillon

PS. Be encouraged

Letters from My Wife

King

Hey Sweetheart I hope and pray that this letter finds you in the best of health and spirit. As we communicate this week the Lord led me to encourage you. I was led to Joshua 1:9 "have not I commanded thee? Be strong and of good courage, be not afraid neither be thou dismayed for the LORD thy God is with the withersoever thou goest." In this particular scripture Moses had passed and the children of Israel were now being led by Joshua. Joshua was encouraging the children of Israel. I am encouraging you on today. Continue to be of good courage, because God is always with you. I am just now realizing that I have not said I love you, not once. I love you! I Miss you more than words can explain. I engaged every moment down to the last second with you. On last visit. I loved how we laid there in the back during our private visit. It gave me a sense of you being home. I just absolutely adore you!

I love you!
Jamara Gillon

Letters from My Wife

King

Hey Sweetheart I hope and pray that this letter finds you in the best of health and spirit. First of all, I just want to say that I miss and love you so much. This week has been very hard! Don't get me wrong. I miss you every day! But sometimes it gets really hard. You are really my best friend and I truly love every moment we spend together. I miss you the very second I leave your presence. You are truly my king; my everything. I can't wait until you come home, and I get to hold you, kiss you, talk to you.

In spite of it all, I will always be there for you waiting until the next time patiently waiting. I love you!

Wifey
Jamara Gillon

Letters from My Wife

King

    Hey Sweetheart I hope and pray that this letter finds you in the best of health and spirit. I know I am not gone do nothing that waste a whole sheet of paper, telling you how much I love you! I miss you so much. You are truly my best friend. I said one of, but you are my only friend. I thank God for you every night. I could not imagine my life without you. I feel truly blessed to have a part of my life. I can't wait until Sunday to see you. We had the best time last visit. We kicked it like we were old friends. I love you dearly! Oh yeah, I'm not pregnant. So keep praying for us. I can't wait to see you. As you can see, I sent you some pictures, but I have so much more to send you. Sorry it took so long. Continue to pray for me, and I will do the same for you! May God bless you. See you and talk to you soon if it is the Lord's will.

                    Your Wife
                 Jamara Asha Dillon

Letters from My Wife

49

King

Hey Sweetheart! How are you? Good I hope! I hope the letter finds you in the best of health and spirit. I'm still so high off our visit this past Saturday. I had such a wonderful time with you. It felt like we were just kicking like we used to do it. When we were in high school. I still can't believe that our 1 year anniversary is just around the corner. It has been such an honor to me to be your wife. It feels totally different from just being your girlfriend. Can't believe we're going 10 years strong. The love just gets better and better. I have to say that you are truly my best friend. I love you with all my heart. It's going to be tough not seeing you for 3 weeks. We done got through it before, so I know we can again. I have shipped that package. Easter of course is this coming up week and everybody supposed to be home. I pray that everything goes well. Keep me in your prayers & I will do the same for you.

Love You, your wife
Jamara Gillon

PS. Dook said, He love you! Kisses & Hugs

Letters from My Wife

King

I hope this letter finds you in the best spirit. Babe I'm really still on cloud 9 from visit. That's just what you do to me! You're truly my best friend. Even Arinton said he can tell our relationship is on another level. Everything is going good. As you can see, Dook behavior has gotten a whole lot better! He growing up. School for me is going good. We had a Christmas break, so I'm having to get back into the swing of things. I love you so much baby. I know that the Lord got so many blessings for us this year. A new life, new city, new addition, and you coming home. I can't wait. LIFE is great and I couldn't ask for nothing more. Baby keep praying for me that I go stronger in the LORD and I will do the same for you.

Love You!
Mrs. Gillon

Letters from My Wife

King

Hey Baby! I miss you and love you so much. There is not a day that goes by that I don't thank God for having you as my husband! I must be special. It's an honor to have you as my husband. I can't wait until Sunday. Just to kiss you and just hold you. I love to be with you just to smell your scent and your warm embrace! Baby I've prayed about doing the fast. I don't think it's the time for us to do the fast. I'm not ready. Thank you so much for being understanding. Baby I can't wait to see you. I need to know before Sunday, can Vamp come with me?

He said his PO approved him. So we're just waiting to hear a word from you. I don't think the girls are going to come! Your grandma said she didn't want them to miss church. They said they gone come home on the 3rd Saturday to come see you! Baby I still haven't got your letter you sent. I don't know what happened. I didn't go to Chap's church. Maybe next time, My funds was low even though I had just got paid! That little 5-9 check was so not enough.

I was kind of sad about my check, but its still a blessing at the same time. Speaking of jobs. I got some good news! They offered me a new position at my job. I'm back full time! I do customer service now. Instead of being on the phone for hours on end. I send mail, receive mail, file important documents, fax, copy, email etc. It's way different than being on this phone hounding people to pay bills.

My shift is 8-5pm Monday - Friday off every weekend. Supposedly after I'm done training I am supposed to start making $9.00 an hour. They supposed to give me a $1 raise. Pray! I'm gone change all my classes to online. That is if my financial aide goes through. It's been problems with my financial aid. I've been calling everyday to see what's up. Really can't nobody tell me why. All of my loans are in deferment and up dated, so I'm not sure. Just pray that everything goes well! My mama said, "Hey." and "She loves you."

Your Wife
Jamara Gillon

Letters from My Wife

PS. Call me before Sunday!

52

King

Hey Baby! I'm the luckiest woman on earth. It just sends chills all over my body to know that God made you specially for me! Just for little old me! I can't wait to spend the rest of my life with you. Sorry I didn't send a card, I was trying to respond to your letter I got before I got your anniversary card. Thank you! Baby. You are so sweet! Words can't express! I know you probably got the letter I sent you, but I had sent it off a day before I got yours, so we kind of butted heads.

Well first off, my most important prayer request is that the LORD send you home between now and the next year, and when you come we can live comfortably. It's a lot of things that I'm trying to do, but it really would be a lot less stressful if you were here. I just want you to be home with me! ASAP! My degree, a job or a house is not more important than being with you. I don't care if we were homeless as long as I'm homeless with you. I wouldn't care. Baby I really feel kind of bad that I turned you down to the fast. I never knew that you had to take away from sex.

I feel kind of selfish! Like I'm holding us up from getting our blessing. I never knew we had to restrain from sex. I thought you just don't eat, read the word for spiritual hunger and thirst and pray. I'm still praying. I love you and hope you're not mad. When are you talking about moving? Everything sounds so good. We keep changing plans. First I will register Dook and me into school. Do you think it would be good to move right now or what? School starts in two weeks. I just started a new job. I don't know. I want to do it. I should have been preparing for it. I feel like if I withdraw from classes here I'm probably gone be too late for registration for me and Dook, which means we sit out another semester. Or I can move, find a good FULL time job, work, wait to let Jerry start school in January. Pre-K does not really count. It just prepares them for kindergarten. In which they have good certified Day cares that have pre-k programs. Day cares are always accepting kids. As far as me, I can always wait until next year for school. It's up to you. your faith is stronger than mine. ON the good side of it all, I am ready to get away from this place anyway! Honestly though I'd really rather talk about all of this in person. We'll talk! I hate I'm not gone get to see you this Sunday! I love you with all my heart.

Your Wife
Jamara Gillon

PS. I love you! I love you! LOL

King

How are you doing? Good I hope. So so sorry that it has taken so long to write you. Honestly I done wrote you like twice before this, but I have yet to get them sent off! My bad, but do understand that I am a very busy woman and have been handling everything I'm supposed to. First of all, you had the right address the first time. I got your letter from your G-Ma! I've handled all that for the marriage. I came up there on last Wednesday. I filled out the papers for our marriage. I sent the $14 money order for your blood test, and I got mine done in Amory. I got to take it back up there within three days. I'm gone do this Wednesday. So all the important stuff is done. The only thing I got to get is our rings! I'm so excited. I can't wait. The apartment is coming along. I haven't moved yet but soon. The lady said the 1st of April, but she has yet to call me. It's so hard to get in touch with her. I can't rush. It will come when it comes.

You know Easter is on the first Sunday which is next week, our visitation day. I am so sad to tell you that I'm not gone come, because it's Easter and your grandma wants us to come. Now if you really want us to come we will. You know I have to obey my husband. It really hurt my heart when I saw that Easter was on 1st Sunday.

Other than business. I'm doing pretty good. My mama & my sister watch DOOK on Saturdays when I work, and they would never charge me to keep him what I spend on daycare a week. I would put him in daycare until he started school in August. I just really don't want to have to depend on nobody for nothing anymore!! When it's all said and done, I love you!

Your wife
Jamara Gillon

PS. Write back ASAP.

Letters from My Wife

55

To my King

Hey Sweetheart! How are things going? Good I hope! Sorry it has taken so long to write! I really do apologize. Honestly though, I have really been busy. I been working so much, 12pm to 9pm so I'm gone from the house for about 10 hours out the day. Even though that's no excuse I've been a work-a-holic. Which I'm not complaining. I'm just always tired. Second, responding to the Last Letter you sent, you said I hurt your feeling when I said you wasn't there to see the things I go through. I never intended to hurt you by saying that. I know you want the best for me, but if you only knew. I am a woman of God. It's only a certain amount of things I can take. It be too much going on in this house that I don't have to take. I know you be worried about my finances, but I'll be ok. Income tax is right around the corner. That is a deposit or down payment. Plus I got so many family members that talking about giving me furniture.

I know you probable worried about me from my last living experience, but I was young, dumb, and inexperienced with handling bills. Even though I didn't make much when I was working there. I still had enough to pay my bills because all my bills was based off my income. I just never managed my money right. I promise I'll be ok. I really do appreciate your concern. That's your job as my man/husband! It's some things that I have to learn on my own. The only place there is left for it to go is up and try again. That's life! That was my first living experience on my own and I messed up but I've learned. I'll be okay bay.. I promise. Don't worry about me so much.

Another thing I'm gone have to work every Saturday from 10am to 7pm. So my visitation day is gone have to be 1st Sunday. So that means I won't get to see you until the 1st Sunday in February. By then I should have my own ride! Hopefully I get paid this Friday, and I'm gone try to send you something and I'm gone try to get a phone. So you can call home! I love you, & don't be mad. Please support me! I love you with all of me. I'm still here for you when you need me!

Your Wife Jamara Gillon
PS. Less than five months
until it is official! Excited!

Letters from My Wife

56

Hey Sweetheart! How are you doing? Good, I hope. I hope this letter finds you in good Spirits! Sorry it took me so long to write you after seeing you on last Saturday! I'm still super excited from the visit, hoping I get to come see you this Sunday. I asked my momma could I drive, and she said that I could if she get a tire for her car. She's got a bad tire. So pray that I do get a chance to come.

Bo said something about me and her taking turns coming, but you know I want to come EVERY VISIT! Am I being selfish? LOL! Let me know because your sisters are soon to be on our visitation list, and I'm not trying to stop that in no kind of way. By the way, that was too sweet of a gift that you got your sisters. Tip read the letter out loud after church too. That was some good teaching. I never knew that you could send stuff like that. Your G-Ma didn't want them to tell who sent them the bible for some reason, but they told me anyway.

On another good note, I Got A Job! for right now it's temporary! It's at a FRED's here in Tupelo. They hired a whole bunch of people, because they need people to set up the store and after that they gone let us go. I went ahead and took it becasue It's convenient. Bo tried to get me hired on with her at Ashley Furniture. The Dude went on and interviewed me, but he said he gone wait to hire me. I'd rather have that job, because I want to be off every weekend, so I can come see you on the weekends. On another note I been doing a lot of grinding like really. Right now I'm working on getting Jeremiah in school for January. If I say to myself I'm becoming a business woman. I have yet to talk to shay or Neal. I saw them again and told them I would call, but when I call no one ever called back. The day I saw them they were with family, and I started to feel like God is really fixing to move mountains. I'm just sitting back patiently waiting. I been looking for a place to stay too. Bo helped me with a few places. So since Kareema let Bo put us in the projects. So since Kareema got a car, Yes I said a Car! Which she bought cash money from her school check. We gone look for some more apartments. So, it's all coming along I can do all thing through Christ which strength me. Phillipains 4:13 Pray for me. I really feel like something good is about to happen. I'm trying to prepare myself, because I know it's gone be too big. I love you! Baby! pray that I get to see you! See you soon!

Your Wife
Jamara Gillon

King

Hey Sweetheart! How are you doing? Good I hope. I miss you so much, and I can't wait to come see you again. Which I don't think we coming to see you this Sunday. You know I'm coming as soon as I get my ride. But Bo said we go come on the next one. Baby Thank you so much for all your advice. I know we laughed about my situation a lot on the last visitation. Which made me feel good. I really was at a low place in my life. I've given it all to God. I'm having a lot of trust issues with people, so I'm putting all my trust in God. After thinking everything through. I think I'm gone stay with Bo. I checked out Hibbetts and they told they would use me as needed. So Bo took me to this place up here in Tupelo, and I really think I got the job. I'm claiming it. I'm not worried about it anymore. I'm deleting everybody out of my life that stopping me from succeeding, or falling short of the glory of God. Whether it's family or friends or anybody. It's time I work on me. My problem is always worrying about how or what other people think about me, or I'm always trying to satisfy everybody. It's time out for that. I'm moving forward from this. I feel a lot better these days. I've been picking up my bible a lot lately and doing a lot of spiritual reading. I'm getting there! I may not be where I used to be! I'm gone get it together Baby. It's just not my time. Just know when it's my time. I'm gone Shine. I love you baby! Pray for us (Me & DOOK)
                    Your Wife
                    Jamara Gillon

Letters from My Wife

59

King

How are you doing, King? Good I hope. Hope this letter finds you in good spirits. Sorry that I wasn't able to come see you this past weekend. It's not very good for me right now. The day before the visit Bo called me, and I told her that Nette wasn't gone be able to meet her. Then Kareema called me later on that night and asked, and told her if Bo would be willing to come get me. It wasn't gone be nothing but an extra 25 minutes drive. She tried to call me early the next day, but I didn't have any minutes on my phone. Everybody doing bad around here. I've had 3 jobs to stand me up. Nette and Dre Bills are high. I try my best not to ask for nothing. I'm getting food stamps so me and Jerry can supply our own food. I know that I've put in over 20 or more applications for jobs since I've been in Memphis, and I'm still unsuccessful. I've been out here grinding hard, and can't nobody tell me I haven't. It's very frustrating. It's a lot of stuff. I need to be doing right now. But it's hard. Like handing the marriage papers. I really need to get to Amory to finish that! But I can't go. Somethings wrong with one of the vehicles. So they only have one vehicle.

Just want you to know I'm trying. It's hard, but I ain't gone give up. I really didn't want to tell you about the situation, because I don't want you to feel like I'm coming up with a million excuses. I would feel guilty if I didn't tell you, because you are my husband, and I have to report everything to you. My spirits are down a little bit right now. I'm human too! You know me. I've always been a little soft. I just want to be successful. Right now I'm feeling like a failure. It's got to be something wrong. If I can't get one job out of 20 or more. Frustrating. Just pray for me. I'm sorry to write you letters like this, because I know it brings you down, and I hate to see you like that. Just be strong for me. Pray harder! Love you!

Your Wife
Jamara Gillon

Letters from My Wife

PS. Thanks for the birthday wishes♡
It turned out good!

Hey Sweetheart!

It is Wednesday. I pray this letter finds you in good health and spirit. I know I'm late sending your pictures, sorry! I am actually writing this letter at the post office. So it will be short. I just want to say I love you dearly, and I had a wonderful visit this past Sunday. The girls said they do intend to come 3rd Saturday. Talk to you Friday. I love you and God Bless you!

Your Wife
Jamara Gillon

Letters from My Wife

Hey Sweetheart!

It is such a blessing to be on this earth one more year. God is so good. He has yet spared us again. Out of your 27 years on this earth. It has been a pleasure spending almost 11 years with you. I hope I have brought a big kookaid smile to your face. I wish you were with me to celebrate grown folks style. LOL. I love you so much, words can't express. I know maybe a card would have been better, but I was trying to time it to get to you on your birthday, and I forgot ya'll don't get mail on Saturdays. So I figured the best and quickest thing was to try out the mail. What I'm trying to say is happy 37th birthday to you. I love you and miss you.

Your Wife
Jamara Gillon

Letters from My Wife

King

Hey sweetheart, I pray this letter finds you in the best health and spirit. I just want to say that I love you with all my heart. I'm still high off our last visit. I've still been thinking of the song you sang for me during our private visit. Your are so sweet. You truly are my best friend. Moving on the business side of things. As you now I'm fixing to get ready to make some decisions on moving and buying furniture. I just ask that you pray for me that I make wise decisions and spend wisely. You know when money is in your hand it can leave so fast. I am ready to make this move. It's time for me and Dook to have our own space. I'm so excited. I love you, and I can't wait to see you. Even though we don't celebrate CUPID, we do celebrate Love. Happy Valentines Day. Kisses & Hugs xoxo.

Your Queen
Jamara Gillon

PS. I love you more than you will ever know

King

Hey sweetheart, It always brings me joy to communicate with you, even by letter. Thanks for my Mother's Day card. I had an amazing time with you this past Saturday. I love to be with you, to be in your presence and just everything about you. I just love you point blank period! It's Monday and I'm missing you like crazy already! I'm counting down the days to see you already. I did send that $40 on your books today. Before Tuesday. So everything should go through. Be in prayer for Jeremiah, he came home from school today complaining his head was hurting. He had a fever of 100 degrees. So be in prayer. Also be praying for your wife. I know I have come a long way in my Christian walk, but it is so much that I still battle with a daily basis. I know the Lord is and already has changed one. I miss you dearly. I just miss you, really miss you! Really Really! Really Miss you! Things just get so tough sometimes, and sometimes I just feel like the world is sitting on my shoulders. I know I can carry it. I just don't want to. On another more positive note. I love you!

Mrs, Datron Gillon

Letters from My Wife

64

King

    I hope this email hits you before the end of the week. Also I pray it brings a smile to your face and joy to your heart. I did not get a chance to even get the pictures printed off this week. My apologies. I just realized that today is Thursday, and I have not wrote you before the week was out. So emailing was the quickest way to get to you. I miss you this week so bad. I was just thinking about our wonderful visit we had last week. We really kicked it like no one else even existed in that visitation room.

    I love every moment I get to spend with you. It is such a blessing like a breath of fresh air. I got your summer package, and I will do it asap. I enjoyed reading your letter this week especially letting me know how overjoyed you felt about how DOOK feel about you. I thought it would kind of bring you down or sadden you a bit. I miss and can't wait to see you and tell you how the LORD blessed me in a major way this week. I love you with all my heart.

Love

Mrs. Datron Gillon

Letters from My Wife

King

Hey my love, I hope this letter is bringing the biggest smile on our face. I know how it feels to get a letter. Seven years in this thing. I still have a huge Kool-Aid smile when I open that mailbox. I know that the day you get this letter, it will not be your birthday, but I hope that you can feel the love and the joy I'm sending your way. I think I may be just as excited for your birthday as you are! When you were born you were created for me, and You didn't even know it. July 14, 1985 is the day my King, lover, husband, best friend and my everything was born. That day will always hold a special day in my heart. I hope and pray you ae happy, and you feel loved. I have been thinking about what you said and thinking this will all be over one day. I can't wait until this is all over, and you are in my arms every day! I love you! Happy Birthday!

Mrs. Datron Gillon

Letters from My Wife

My Love,

Hey my love. I miss you and love you very much. I cannot wait to see you. By the time you receive this letter. I'll be less than 24 hours from seeing you. I have really enjoyed reading your letters this week. You bring a smile to my face every time I open the mailbox and see that handwriting. It is just a blessing to be on your mind, let alone be in your presence. This has been a long week, and I feel like I have not seen you in a long time. I miss you so much. I have been counting down the days to see you. I am still so super proud of your accomplishments in almost completing your degree. I just wish you were on your way home so we could celebrate. Well my word limit is running out, so I will talk to you tomorrow. Sending you all my love and kisses. Love you!

Mrs. Datron Devaugh Gillon

Letters from My Wife

King

Hey my love. I hope this letter brings a blessing to your life today. I miss you sooo much. Thank God. I hope you hold up your end of the bargain. I cannot wait to feel your arms around me. I love you so much and truly enjoyed our family time we got in last week with Dook being there. I have really missed you this week. There is so much to talk about with this car deal situation. Well I will tell you this... for right now I do not have the car. I will have to explain it to you later. I should get my paycheck in my account on Friday. I can put some money on your phone so you can call. If the call do not go through, just know that I did not get my check. If I do not get it on Friday. I will have to first thing Saturday morning, and I will put the money on the phone early Saturday. So try both times. I love and can't wait to see you. I got the numbers and addresses you needed.

Vamp got your letter and texted me this big long text of apology and your grandma called after she talked to you Sunday. I will fill you in on everything Saturday. This has been a tough week, but I yet made it. God is good! Love you! Miss You!

Mrs. Datron Gillon

Letters from My Wife

King

Hey love. I pray that this email finds you in the best health and spirits. I got your letter on Tuesday and some of the same things you talked about. I was thinking. I loved how we communicated with one another. It may have had some high and low parts, but it was much needed. I was writing you back on paper and realized I did not have any more stamps. I decided to write you through email, so it would reach you before the week is out. I love you, and this past visit got me feeling some type of way too. It just shows growth and how much we have grown. You really bring the best out of me. Sometimes I do not always see the best in myself, but that is what we have each other for. God bless you and have a great day. Talk to you soon. I know this was a short letter, but it is sweet... love you.

J Gillon

Letters from My Wife

King

    Today is Thursday, and I just got your letter in the mail. No need to apologize for being late. I am always late. So you can stand to be late once or twice LOL. I miss you so much. Yet I feel that the feeling of missing you is going to soon be over. I have had a few problems with DOOK this past week, but I am still working hard on him. I will tell you all about it Saturday. This week for me has been kind of touch. Coming off from spring break last week to the time changing has made me feel really tired. I also got to tell you how a six year old student stole my phone at work. I love you, and I cannot wait to see you. I will be myself this weekend. I need all of your attention. Love you babe. Be encouraged. I am yet praying!

                  Your Wife
                  Jamara Gillon

Letters from My Wife

King

My love... I hope and pray that this letter finds you in the best health and spirit. I was just reading your letter, and I noticed how you listen to me. It is a blessing to sit back and watch our marriage blossom. It just hit me that this is a fifth weekend. I am so sad. Like really I am really going to miss you more. I pray you get this letter on time. I want you to wait until Saturday to call me. I am trying to get some other things straightened out, so there won't be any money on the phone until then. I love you. Continue to pray for me. I am praying for you.

Your Wife
Jamara Gillon

Letters from My Wife

My Love

   I hope and pray that this email finds you in great health and spirit. What a blessing it is to be communicating with you. It is like a breath of fresh air. I hope that you have had a great week. I have been on the countdown every since I left you on the last Saturday. We are literally hours away from seeing each other. I have missed you something terrible. I love being around you, because it seems as if nothing else exist. I know exactly what it is. It is nothing but God that keeps us as close as we are, and I am thankful. I am sorry that I have been slothful in writing you. It has been a lot going on. I am going to try to have money on the phone by tonight. If not then just know I tried. I am trying to see if I will have anything extra to go to Amory this weekend and next weekend. This weekend is the railroad festival and next week is Easter. So my budget is tight. So if I do not talk to you tonight. I will see you tomorrow. I love you, and God bless you. I hope you get this email on time. Love, Pray. Love. Believe.
                    Your Wife
                    Jamara Gillon

Letters from My Wife

King

Hey my love. What a pleasure it is to be writing you. I really missed you this past week. I hope and pray that this letter finds you in great health and spirit. I have really been thinking this week on how much I admire the man you have become. You have truly become the man that I have always looked up to. You are really a great leader. I know when you come home, you are going to be the best husband ever. I have no doubts. You have proven to me that you are ready to come home. That shows how much my faith is in God. All my prayers for you have come into fruition. I love you. I adore you. There may not be any money on the phone Friday, but try anyway. We are supposed to go to Amory this weekend. Also I am going to get you those pictures as soon as possible. It's not going to be this week though, sorry. I love you so much! God bless you!

Your Wife
Jamara Gillon

Letters from My Wife

Happy Anniversary

My love. Do you know what today is? It's our anniversary. What a blessing and an honor it is to be called your wife. Your have given me the best four years of my life even in our circumstances. I feel like those women in the bible days who loved and honored their husbands despite what the circumstances were. Beyonce asked a question. Who wants the perfect love story anyway, or who wants the hero love that saves the day. I do and I found that in you. I am blessed. I do want you to know that I appreciate your gift to me Saturday, even though I was embarrassed. That let me know how much you love me. Most men in the free world do not do that for their wives. These four year have really flown by. They say time really flies when you are having fun and I am having the time of my life. I love you baby and happy fourth anniversary. My love and my king this is just the beginning. We have so much more to look forward to. Whoso findeth a wife findeth a good thing and obtaineth favour of the Lord. Baby you got favor. Be blessed and pray for me as I pray for you. Love you.

Your Wife

Jamara Gillon

Letters from My Wife

My Love

It's been a minute since I actually wrote you. I must admit actual writing feels more personal. I am actually late getting these pictures sent off. I have had a toothache from hades this week. I finally got an appointment tomorrow 5-9-14. I know by the time you get this letter I will have already talked to you and seen you. I apologize for my slothfulness. I miss you like crazy this week. It was really good to hear from you on Tuesday. I needed that. I know you are smiling from ear to ear for your pictures. Sorry it took so long. I love you, and I'll be seeing you soon my love. Enjoy your pictures. I know the importance of seeing these milestone. Pray. Love. Believe.

The Wife
Mrs. Datron Gillon

PS. Love you to the moon and back! xoxo

Letters from My Wife

King

My love I pray that this letter finds you in great health and spirit. Today is Thursdays June 5, 2014. I got your letter yesterday. I want to go ahead and tell you that Dook will be coming this weekend. My sister has plans. So he has no choice. We always can have "us" time with or without Dook being there. Boy this has been the longest two weeks of my life. Feels like I haven't seen you in ages. I miss you, and I cannot wait to put my hands around your handsome face to kiss you and hug you, to be in your warm embrace. I've been doing a lot of thinking about when you come home. Just on how we are going to be with one another, the church, and family and friends. What a joyous occasion. I'm so ready for that day. It's been a long time coming and our journey will soon be over. Pray for me as I continue to pray for you. Love you Mr. Gillon. Be blessed!

The Wife
Mrs. Datron Gillon

PS. I love you more than you'll ever know. God was thinking of me when he made you. It's an honor and a privilege to watch you grow into the man I always wanted. I'm blessed.

Letters from My Wife

King

    I want to tell you how deeply sorry I am for not making it to your MRT graduation. I'm just as hurt for not being able to make it as you are. Today is Thursday 12-11-2014, I'm feeling worse than yesterday. I don't believe I am going to make it another week with this tooth in my mouth on top of Aunt Flow being in town. This has been an awfull week. I'm making it. It's almost over I hope you understand. When I looked at the clock at one today. I was trying to imagine how you felt without seeing me there. I was there in Spirit, and so Was the Lord. So you were really not alone. I love you and thank you for understanding hopefully. I love you!

                    The Wife
                    Mrs. Datron Gillon

Letters from My Wife

King

My love, Happy New year!! What A blessing it is to be entering into another year with you. We have been together almost half of our lives. I'm so happy. Time is winding down & soon you will be home with us and our family will be complete. I have been sitting back all week reflecting on our last visit. We really be kicking it like best friends. We use shaking hands like we are best buddies.

I absolutely love our bond that we have. I truly adore you. Can you believe that it is about to be 2015? Man! Time waits on no one. That's why when you come home, I want us to travel so when we're older we can sit and reflect on the past. I love you so much! Can't wait to see you Saturday!
Love Mrs. G

PS. It's a G-Thang

The Wife
Mrs. Datron Gillon

Letters from My Wife

My King

My love I just got your letter and it immediately put a smile on my face. I pray that this letter does the same for you. I want to address something you wrote in your letter to me. [You said you were so hurt about me discussing that situation with our friend.] Well first of all, I feel like you have jumped the gun a little bit. Well at the last visit, not this past one, but the one before. I asked you about that situation and you said no! Our friend called me after I discussed it with you to check on me and to see if I had got the boots exchanged. He is the one who said you need some protection. I immediately told him I had already talked to you about it, and you said no. So at visit he made it seem like I had him to check on it.

You never gave me a chance to explain! That makes me feel like you have no trust that I would come to you first about everything. [In which I do] I hope that clears that up! On another note I really enjoyed myself with you. You are an amazing man. I feel like I am so blessed to have a God fearing man who reverence God in every aspect of life. I I know everything you lead me to do is out of love. It may be a little hard for me to accept sometimes, but I ask for your patience. Sometimes your delivery is VERY STRONG and that's why I may take it that way, because of your delivery. I love you and I am praying harder than ever for us to finally be together as a family unit. I miss you. I'm getting really sad that our private visit are about to be over! I love you. Talk to you and see you soon!
Your Wife
J. Gillon

PS. There is still no money on the phone

Letters from My Wife

79

My King

Well it's Tuesday and I'm back from Chiraq (Chicago). We had, well I had a wonderful time! We actually got back late Sunday. We had to cut our trip short because of money situations. It was a good trip though, and boy did I miss you! I know you said you were not going to call me on my trip, but honestly I didn't believe you. P)lease don't do that again. Hearing your voice would have at least eased the pain of missing you so much. I'm missing you something serious. I tell you I'm counting down the days to Saturday. I don't have pictures yet but I have them on my phone. I'll send them soon! Also Brother Kurt called, and said he need to hear from you. You are the only one he don't hear from. I love you dearly & miss you! I can't wait until I see you to tell you all about my trip!

Love You
Mrs. D Gillon

Letters from My Wife

My Love, My King, My Everything

I hope and pray that this letter finds you in great health and spirit, along with a huge smile on your face straight to the point. Got home Saturday and Dook is normal as he want to be. I immediately thought, Dang! I could have stayed longer. But getting one minute with you is better than none at all. I got some news back finally from Chickasaw County, but it is not great. We'll talk more Friday. Also this Friday the 14th, your grandma wants me to come home to support her in a program she will be preaching. I kind of want to go, but don't want to. I'm torn because she wants me to stay and miss seeing you. That is something we haven't really discussed or came to an agreement on. I don't know right now. The prison ministry program went really well this weekend. So many of your old friends were there. It was so encouraging to see those guys get out and be successful and blessed. I love it! I will talk to you soon!

Wifey
J. Gillon
Love you dearly

PS. Icky said don't forget his visitation form

Letters from My Wife

My Love

    I want to start off by saying I love you. I hope and pray that this letter finds you in great health and spirit. Boy oh Boy do I miss you. These two weeks have been the longest ever, but I'm so happy that the countdown is almost over. I went ahead and signed Dook up for basketball. Hopefully this will help with some of the behavior. I did tell him that if he don't show improvement that I will take him off the team, regardless if I have already paid. It's been tough dealing with this on my own. But in the last week, I have seen some improvement enough of Dook. I can't wait to see you. These two weeks have been difficult. Seeing you every week is what gets me by. I love you! I miss you. Talk to you soon!

                Mrs. Gillon

Letters from My Wife

My King

First and foremost, I want to apologize for not writing you as often as I should. I know that you get just as excited as I do to get mail from you. I also want to apologize for the negative attitude. I had at visit this past Saturday. I know that you was just trying to keep me encouraged and the Word is the only thing that will stick. To be honest and "no excuses" my emotions were all over the place! I do have to consider your emotions as well. I got your letter today and it put a smile on my face. I know that God has my back. He allowed me not to be at home when it happened. That was His protection! Material things come and go God has already given me a peace of mind. I'm still extra careful but I'm not losing sleep. I also had an amazing time just laying there with you. I feel so safe with you! I can't wait until you get here. The countdown begins! I love you! Can't wait until Saturday so I can get my hands on you and get some sugar.

Love your wife
J Gillon

Letters from My Wife

My Love

    I know you don't like to celebrate birthdays anymore, but I will forever celebrate 7-14-1985. To me, even though I was not born yet, was the best day of my life. A king was born and all of you belongs to me. Now tell me that doesn't call for a celebration. LOL. I love you so much baby. Happy 32nd Birthday!

Mrs. J Gillon

xoxo

Letters from My Wife

My Love

I love you, and that is all I really want to let you know in this letter. I love you and all I want to do is love you. I've been praying fervently about our marriage. Though we have gotten a whole lot better at communicating. I feel like we have to try so hard sometimes to be on the same page. I just wish it was easier. Maybe this is just the growing stage, and it is necessary to go through it to be better. I just want to focus on keeping the Lord at the center of our marriage. I love you dearly. You are still the man of my dreams. Thank you baby for even trying to be the best you. I see how far we've come at talking and how far we can go. Thank you for being who you are, I love you and miss you.

Mrs. J Gillon
XOXO

Letters from My Wife

My Love

    I have been thinking about you non-stop since visit. I just feel like I've fallen in love with you all over again! Not that I've fallen out, it's just a great feeling to be back in a good space! I genuinely apologize for the way I've acted towards you. No excuses. I built a wall up against you for personal reasons and allowed the devil to enter into our marriage. You have to realize it in order to make a change. I'm just glad the Lord showed me! I love you so much babe! You mean the world to me! I appreciate the man you are! I'm so thankful to you and feel so blessed to call you my husband. You are Everything that a wife could ask for. I mean that from the bottom of my heart! I love you dearly! Talk to you soon!

Mrs. J Gillon
xoxo

Letters from My Wife

My Love

    I hope and pray that this letter finds you in great health and spirit. I hope that you have the biggest smile on your face right now. Knowing this gives me great joy. Monday and Tuesday passed me by so quickly, but I was determined to get you a letter before the week was out. Today is Wednesday and my week has been ok. Just ok. Nothing bad has happened or anything. I'm just tired. Monday I spent the day unpacking, washing, and organizing clothes in the closet. Jeremiah also had basketball practice at 6pm. Tuesday I worked until 6pm and went to my nephew's basketball game. They played Olive Branch High School and lost. We finally made it to the house around 9:30pm. I showered and passed out. I'm actually at work on my planning period. I have been thinking of you heavily since our visit on Sunday. I just want you to know that I hear you. I promise I do. I also want you to know that I love you. I want you to know it, see it, feel it, and breathe it. I hate the fact that you don't see it as much as you'd like to, but I'm going to do my best in showing you. I love you times infinity! Hugs and kisses.

                XOXO
           Mrs. Gillon

Letters from My Wife

King

Hello my love. Straight to the business. If possible please send me the dates of all of your medical request. Your mom, Bo, and G-ma are all worried about you and have been calling. I'm gone try to make it there early this Saturday, because I need to leave early. This is the birthday dinner they're having for Grandma, starting at 2. Also no money will be on the phone again this week. Sorry for this short quick letter. I was trying to get this out quick.

Love
Mrs. Gillon

Letters from My Wife

My Love

I hope and pray that this letter lifts your spirits higher. I have been thinking of you heavily. Just want you to know that I love you. Though we had a descent visit Saturday overall, and I have forgiven you. I do want to know why you quit your job? Just a simple question. Don't try to read more into it. I pray that you have had a blessed week. I want you to know that I pray for you daily. I pray that God continues to strengthen you. I pray that you continue to be the man that I have always prayed for. You are amazing. I truly want to say thank you for being you. Even when you make mistakes, you man up, apologize, and try to do better. I'm grateful for you. I honestly want you to know that I see you. I love you! Continue to pray for me, I need it. I got some not so great news about the apartment. I'll talk to you about it at visit. Love you!

Your Wife
Mrs. Gillon

PS. Please tell Jessie Thanks for the encouragement!

Letters from My Wife

My Love

    I had an amazing time with you this past visit. We had a bump in the road, but we were able to work it out, which is amazing. Because we know there was a time that it seemed like we couldn't talk it out. I admire you for your growth and understanding. I'm still praying for you daily just as you are praying for me. Calvin was able to get my car fixed. Praise God! You know what I thank God for the most? Is you getting your friends to send people to help. Brother Kurt called. Jessie was calling his folks. I felt so blessed, and I Immediately asked God to forgive me, because I'm never alone! Thank you for that. Love you baby!

                XOXO
                Mrs. Gillon

Letters from My Wife

My Love

I'm feeling some type of way right now just to be writing you. I had an amazing time with you this past Saturday. We had an awesome time with the family this weekend. It went by so fast. I'll be back to the basics this week. There are no more breaks until summer. Pray for me. I am going to be working really hard these next eight weeks. Just pray that the Lord gives me all the strength I need to get by. Also I want you to pray that those summer jobs come through. I love you so much, my love, and I miss you already. I want you to know that I sold the car. I was only able to get $700 for it, because there were some other problems going on with it. I didn't have that male support, So I was desperate. My mom felt that it was reasonable. I only paid $1200 for it and a transmission is anywhere from $500-$1000. So I'm not tripping. I love you. See you soon!

J Gillon

My Love

   Hey sweetheart! I love you more than you will ever know. No words in the Webster can describe the true way I feel about you. Just had to start this letter off that way! I'm honestly still high off of our last visit. I'm always so blessed and delighted to be in your presence. I know in my heart that you were heaven sent, and we were created for each other. I feel so blessed. Everyday I wake up. I literally count down the days until I see you again. I was just sitting here thinking earlier today that I couldn't wait until this week is over, so I can see you again. I was also thinking after this year, we got one more year. If it's the Lord's will. Praying. God has not failed me yet. I know He will never fail me! I'm sorry my letter is late for Valentines, and sorry there is still no pictures. Sometimes I feel there is not enough time.
                              J Gillon

Letters from My Wife

My Love

   You talking about being on an emotional high right now! I enjoyed every second with you at visit! You were giving me those looks that told every secret. You are truly my best friend! It was so necessary for us to go through those debates, because it in turn made the relationship stronger and better. If you can overcome them! We did! I thank God for you everyday. I hear stories of women going through so many different changes in their relationship, but you adore me! For that, I love you! Just for being you, I love you! I miss you so much! Thank God we are less than a year away from being together! I love you babe! Have a blessed week! Pray for me as I will for you!

                              Mrs. Gillon

Letters from My Wife

My Love

Lately I have been studying scriptures of the role of the husband. It was part of a devotional that caught my attention. The first scripture was I Timothy 5:8 "But if any provide not for his own and specially for those of his own house, he hath denied the faith and is worse than an infidel." This scripture talks about the role of the husband starting with leadership, but encompasses provision and protection. He must protect her physically, mentally, and spiritually. This brings me to my next scripture. I Peter 3:7 "likewise ye husbands dwell with them according to knowledge, giving honor unto the wife as until the weaker vessel and as being heirs together of the grace of life. That your prayers be not hindered."

This scripture puzzled me for a minute until I further read the commentary. It says women are physically weaker than the man, but through grace our ultimate goal is to be joint heirs. So we are to be treated as equal because in our new life we will be equals. Husbands are instructed to do this, so they're prayers aren't hindered. My final scripture I want to share is Ephesians 5:25-33. "Husbands love your wives just as Christ loved the church and gave himself for it. That he may sanctify and cleanse it with the washing of water by the word." This is one of the most important to me! Loving your wife as Christ loves us! Loving your wife as you love yourself! Cleansing your wife with the word. Helping her to be a better her, the same as you do with yourself. So you can present me without blemish. I just wanted to share with you what I've been studying to encourage you to continue to be the best husband that you are. Next, I'll be studying the role of the wife. I will share with you what I've learned. Be encouraged my love! Eight more months! I love you dearly!

XOXO
Mrs. Gillon

Letters from My Wife

My Love

   I love you! What better way to start off a letter to the one that I love. Did you know that I love you? Like really? Almost 16 years later, and you are still the man of my dreams! I pray that this letter finds you in the best health and spirit. I just want you to know that you are simply amazing. Thank you for opening up to me and sharing your feelings on the impact of not having your dad a part of your life. I know that wasn't easy, putting those emotions out there. I really admire that in you. Like I said, you and Clyde are both still alive, so there is an opportunity to get it right between ya'll. Be open to just asking him those tough questions, but also be willing to receive an answer and willing to forgive. My pen went out lol. Just be encouraged. You know that nothing is too hard for God. I know of a surety that God mends relationships. I will be praying on that. I love you my king. Keep your head up. Five and a half months left! God is good! I love you!

Mrs. Gillon
XOXO

Letters from My Wife

My Love

    I just want to start off by saying that I hope and pray that this letter finds you in the best of health and spirit. I love you so much baby. You should see the smile on my face right now as I'm writing. It brings so much joy to my heart to know that you're mine and that you will be home in 5 months! Baby the countdown is real! LOL! This space that we're in right now brings so much peace to me. I'm just filled with joy. I don't even know what to say. I feel like I'm being repetitive. I do love you and miss you!

                   Mrs. Gillon
                   XOXO

Letters from My Wife

My Love

    It's Monday night. I just got done reading my devotional, and you are on my mind heavily. Thank you for the conversation that we had on Sunday. I know that I didn't say much, but I was listening. I really took what you said to heart. I am trusting and believing that everything is working for our good. I apologize for not getting a letter out in over a week. I'm trying to get back on track. I think I've made up my mind about going to Florida. I don't think it's a good idea to go at this time because of school starting back. It's rent time again. It's just not a good time financially. I hate that I'm going to miss this opportunity to relax, but I have too much to do to be out of town right before school starts! I'm okay in knowing that it won't always be like this!

    Thank you so much baby for the man that you are! I appreciate you for being a great leader, which in turn makes it so easy to follow. You inspire me to be a better person. I love the way you encourage me, motivate me, pray for me, and Love me! I love you for that! Until next time.

XOXO

Jamara Gillon

PS. Be encouraged My Love, Only a few more months!

Letters from My Wife

97

My Love

You are simply amazing, and I love you forever! Thank you for being who you are to me! I can only imagine what it's going to be like when you get home. You'll call and I'll say, "Baby I need help" or "Baby I want or need!" Even from behind prison walls, you're trying to make it happen! I may not show it all of the time, but I appreciate you. I love you for that. I sometimes hate to put that pressure on you, because I know that sometimes you can't get what you need done. I know all too well, what it feels like to want to help, but can't. Please forgive me for not asking Vamp. I couldn't bring myself to do it. So I got those bills rearranged and got a little spending money from my sister. I love you. Thank you so much for all you do for me. I may as well just stop trying to fight it, because I know when you come home it's over with. Spending this time with you this past weekend made me fall deeper in love with you. If that's possible. I miss you terribly already! I told Dook no more options on coming to visit. I told him that you need him there for these last few months. He said he loves you, and so do I!

Mrs. Gillon

XOXO

Letters from My Wife

My Love

I really would like to apologize for not writing like I should. I can do better, no excuses. I also want to let you know how much I love you, and I'm truly thankful for the man you have become. I feel like I don't express that enough to you. I'm really proud! Honestly! I hope these pictures put a smile on your face baby. We are literally months away from all of this being a memory of the past. Can't wait! I'm going to try to have money on the phone Friday. Finances been a little tight. Be praying for me. I know you already do, and that's why I'm maintaining now. I know it's you who's praying harder for me more than you pray for yourself. I love you! Mr. Gillon, Love you babe!

Mrs. Gillon

XOXO

Letters from My Wife

King

He may not always be there when you call, but He is always on time. I'm so sorry it took so long for you to get your pictures. But here we go. I hope these memories bring you great joy! Happy Holidays. It's amazing to know this Christmas is the last one alone, finally. I miss you terribly! I love you with every inch of me. I'm going to make you a happy man when you come home. I love you & can't wait to see you.
Mrs. Gillon
XOXOXO

Letters from My Wife

My Love

    I know I have not written you in a while, but baby please don't charge it to my heat! There is not a day that goes by that I don't think about you. As a matter of fact, I carry your spirit with me daily. Your smile your intelligent words, your passion and just everything about you gets me through each day. I am missing you terribly right now. I love you more than any word could express right now. Baby we are three and a half months away from seeing each other everyday. All this not seeing each other will be a thing of the past. Thank you baby for allowing God to use you and for loving me the way you do. I'm blessed to have you as my husband. Not every woman can say that! Hope I see you soon or at least talk to you.

        Love you & Miss you!
        Mrs. Gillon

Letters from My Wife

My Love

    I just want to say that I love you unconditionally! You make me so happy! Your are still the man of my dreams. I'm still high off our past visit which started off rough, but ended so well. I wanted to kiss you the whole time. That's what you do to me. The same man can bring out ten different emotions in 6 hours. I went from being mad at you, only in the 1st hour, to laughing with you, to wanting to take you down right there on the table. I love you dearly. Thinking of you makes my heart happy. You make me happy! I'm so in love with you and proud to call you my husband. We only have 8 more visits before you come home., Four weekends in February. It's five weekends in March so no visit the weekend before you come home. Eight more visits!!! Then I can get all the loving I want!! I miss you. Be encouraged. I love you.
               XOXO
               Mrs. Gillon

Letters from My Wife

My Love

Hey Love, just been vibing to this song for a while now. Lauren Hill was the absolute truth. It's reminding me so much of what we have. Our Love. which is the sweetest thing I know. I love you so much. I'm literally counting down the days man! It's breathtaking to know how life in the near future is going to be. That's what keeps me going. The Lord has revealed so much to me about our marriage. I'm really in my feelings right now and counting down the days to see you. When I'm with you nothing else matters. It's like I get to be myself. It's like I'm someone else playing a character in a movie when I'm not with you. Thirteen years and I still get nervous, shy, and then comfortable every time I see you. We really have something special. Blessed to say the least! I love you so so so much!

XOXO
Mrs. D. Gillon

Letters from My Wife

www.ingramcontent.com/pod-product-compliance
Lightning Source LLC
Chambersburg PA
CBHW071024120626
46546CB00003B/1208

* 9 7 8 1 9 6 0 8 5 3 5 8 5 *